This Book Belongs to

ISBN: 9781961902657

In a jungle so green, under skies big and blue,
Zen Monkey swings where banana trees grew.
He shares his treats, with a grin so wide,
But keeps his own branch, with no one to collide.

A loud bird squawks, filling the air,
Zen Monkey says, "Please talk soft, be fair.
My branch is for quiet, my place to rest,
You can have the next one, it's just as best!"

"Let things go," Zen Monkey shows with play,
"Like leaves that float down and then fly away.
Drop what is heavy, what makes you frown,
And you'll feel as light as a feather blown down."

Squirrel with her nut, looks for a spot to stash,
Monkey says, "Save some, or it'll be gone in a flash.
But when nuts are too many, just let them roll,
Like clouds in the sky, letting go is the goal."

A butterfly trapped, in a hand that's too close,
Monkey says, "Set it free, it will thank you the most."
When it flutters away, in the warm sunlight,
Monkey smiles, "Letting go feels so right."

"Boundaries keep us happy, like fish in the sea,
Saying where we start and where others will be."
Monkey jumps in the air, then lands with a twirl,
"See, everyone's space is their own little world."

To friends who come close, with a high-five or a spin,
Monkey says, "This is where I end, and you begin."
Letting go of things, like a vine or a ball,
Is easy to do and fun for us all.

In the jungle, the sun rises with each new day,
And Zen Monkey knows just how to play.
With space for himself and things left behind,
He finds joy in each moment, with peace of mind.

He watches the river, how freely it flows,
"Water moves on, wherever it goes."
Like the river, he learns, we can hold or set free,
Just as nature shows with each rock and tree.

With every new morning, to his jungle friends' delight,
Zen Monkey wakes up and bathes in the light.
"Good boundaries," he says, "make good friends, too,
They help us feel safe in whatever we do."

He teaches thc birds, and the bees that buzz,
That each has a place, and that's just because
They need room to live, to fly, and to grow,
To buzz and to fly high and low.

At snack time he nibbles, on a fruit so sweet,
Zen Monkey thinks sharing is a treat.
"But when I'm full, I'll say 'No, thank you,'
And save some for later, it's easy to do."

The sun dips low, and the moon climbs high,
Zen Monkey knows it's time to sigh.
"Time for me, and time for you,
To rest, to dream, under the sky so blue."

In the heart of the jungle, where life's so grand,
Zen Monkey's happy with his small piece of land.
With a place of his own, and friends so dear,
He's full of love, with nothing to fear.

The stars twinkle down, with stories to tell,
Of a monkey who knows boundaries and letting go well.
With a happy heart and a spirit so free,
Zen Monkey's life is a joy, you see.